efghijklmnopqrstuvwxyz. 012

Aa Bb Cc Dd Ee Ff Gg Hh Ii Jj Kk

the quick brown fox. aaa bbb ccc ddd

Qq Rr Ss Tt Zz3 ... Oo P

Ll Mm Nn O lazy dog !

abcdefghijklmnopqrstuvwxyz. yyy 33

0123456789. Aa Bb Cc Dd Ee Ff Gg Hh

Ii Jj Kk Ll Mm Nn Oo Pp Qq Rr Ss Tt Uu Vv

ee fff ggg hhh the, in, an, penmanship ...

THE WORDSMITH
BY JANET CLARE

(n.) one who creates with words

To Marion love

for my keys, as everything is Janet Clare

WELCOME

I've often wished that I kept a diary or an art journal but after many attempts I've had to admit that I'm just not that sort. And yet, I really do want to remember and record our ordinary days. After all, what you do every day is more important than what you do once in a blue moon.

One day I realised that I could simply stitch our stories and here we are. 'The Wordsmith' is about noticing and cherishing the simple things in life. It's about slowing down, quietening the mind and finding the joy in the mundane; gathering your memories and mementoes together with beautiful fabrics and soothing stitches to create a lasting cloth to be talked over and treasured by generations to come: a quilted memory to cherish.

So come, gather your letters and your threads and be a wordsmith with me.

Janet x

A wordsmith simply must have an alphabet to work with, and so here is ours.

The alphabet quilt

A.S
57

We live almost under the flight path of a small airport

and rather than complain about
all the ado we've decided instead
to notice and appreciate the
aeroplanes - to make them a
bustling feature of the garden.

ADO

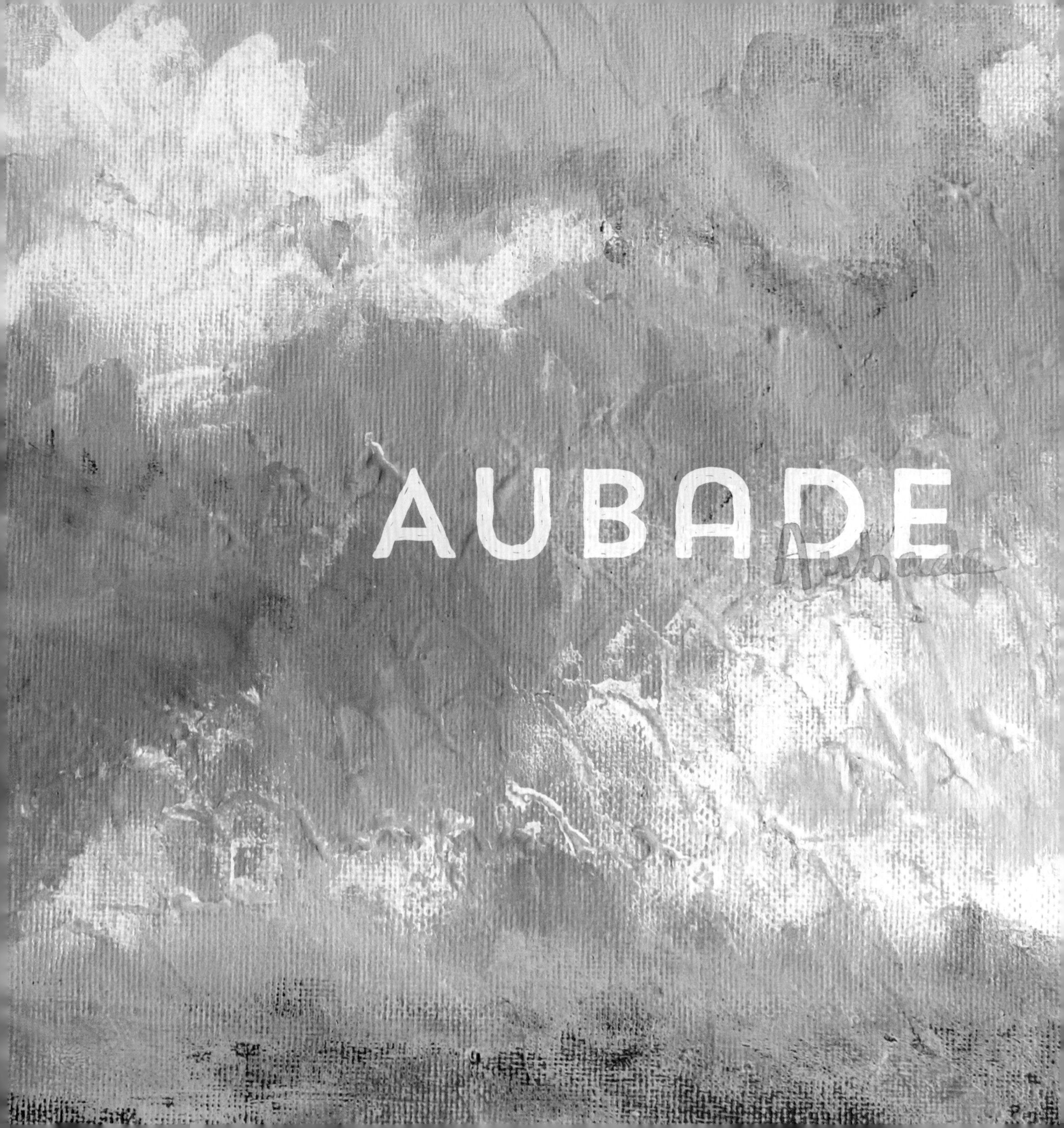
AUBADE

(n) a love song to the dawn

'B' is for budgie in braille on Broderie Anglaise

We saw the New Year in with good friends,
bubbly, a balloon modelling competition and
Gary Barlow (our god-daughters' budgie).

I don't do meditation, or yoga or lying in the sun.
I've tried repeatedly but being still bores me to tears.
If I need to calm down and simply 'be' I paint, stitch,
knit or bake. It's only when my hands are busy
that my whirring brain and I truly relax.

BLOSSOM BY HENRY, AGE 9

Old crumbly branches
hang elegantly over me
swaying the beautiful pink
buds side to side

cake · coffee ·
champagne ·
cheese · 🐓 ·
· chips
· chocolate ·
crisps ·

comatose.

SIT

STAY

COME

A combination of reading about the Dickin Medal (awarded to heroic animals) and a long dull evening sewing Scout badges onto uniforms got me thinking about the 'decorations' Betty would be awarded. This is about it (on a good day).

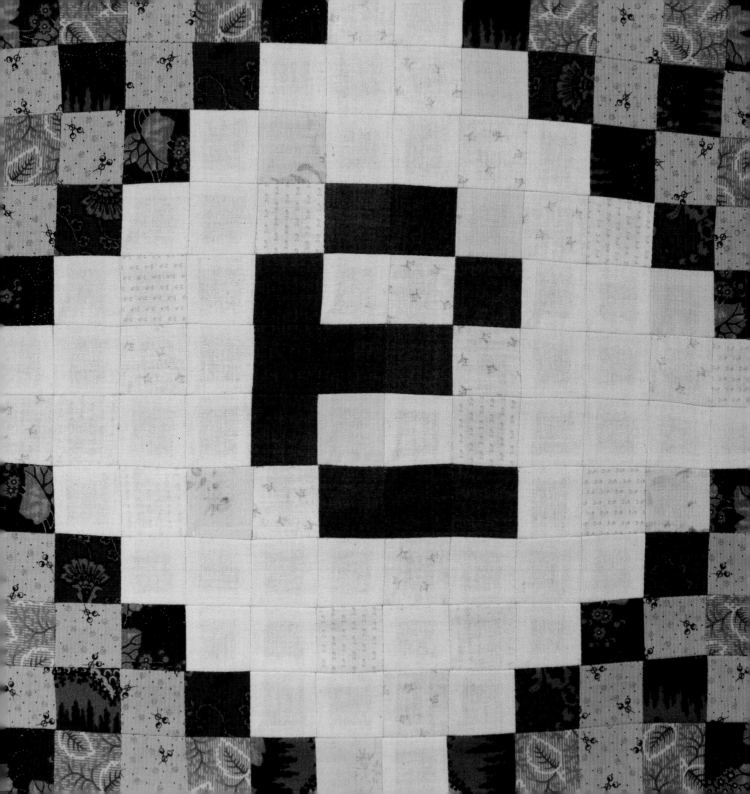

Satin stitch for leaves

large single chain stitches?

hand quilted background

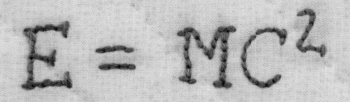

$$E = MC^2$$

E is for energy and Einstein and my husband
who studied physics and actually understands
such things. All I really know about energy is
that much in life depends on it.

I can't even remember learning how to sew,
to embroider, to use a needle and thread;
it feels like something I've always just known.
I do remember my Mum, my Granny and
my Aunties sitting chatting with busy hands
working away, so I must have been shown
the basics and absorbed the rest.

I remember my Granny's tin with the
yellow roses on where she kept her
embroidery silks all neatly wrapped round
little pieces of card. And I remember digging
my fingers deep into her button tin.

Now both my boys can sew and seem to have
learnt the same way I did, by absorption.

In a word; football. My life revolves around it. If they're not watching it, they're playing it or I'm washing their kits. Joe gave me a running commentary as he was drawing this and I taught him a new word,

FERVENT

in fine fettle

So, we have a Greenfinch in our freezer...

The poor thing was discovered dead on the crazy golf course and brought home in our picnic box. The boys have plans to taxidermy it when they're older.

The poor thing was discovered dead on the crazy golf course and brought home in our picnic box. The boys have plans to taxidermy it when they're older.

Gumption

(n.) spirited, shrewd initiative and resourcefulness

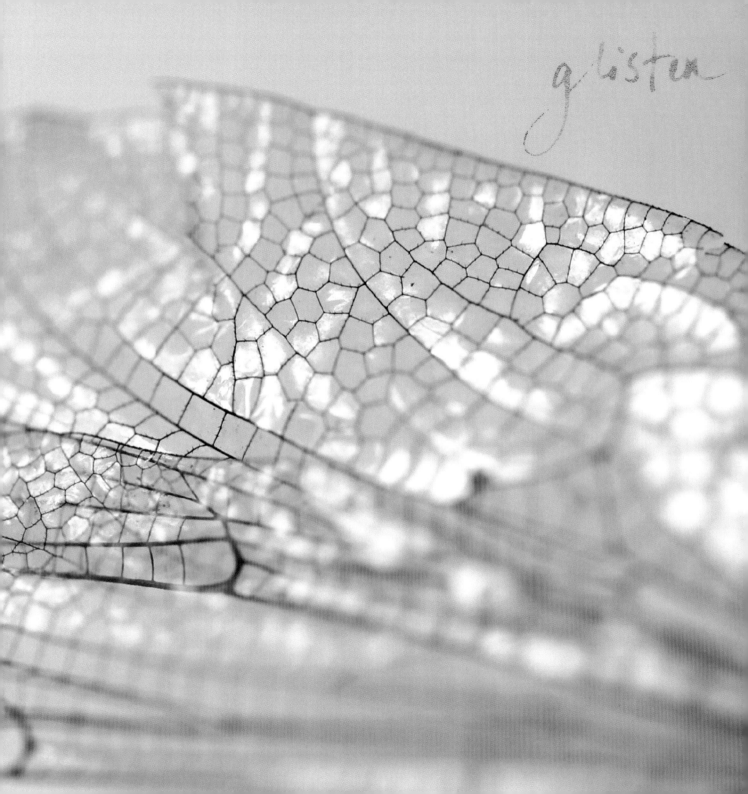

glisten

There is only one thing H could be about and that is my lovely son, Henry.

Henry

ICHTHYOSAUR

We all enjoy a spot of fossil hunting on Charmouth Beach, Dorset when we are visiting our country friends who live nearby. The beach is famous for its fossils particularly in the winter months when the rough seas help to churn them up. So, a day fossil hunting is almost guaranteed to be a cold, damp and windswept one.

After a while of peering fruitlessly into rock pools and shingly piles you 'get your eye in' and suddenly there are Belemnites and Ammonite fragments everywhere you look. In fact, they are so plentiful you can even afford to be choosy about which ones you take home with you.

But, my story is about one never to be forgotten day when I found something small and hexagonal-ish which had a smooth dent in the centre on both sides. I knew I had found a 'something'. I put it in my pocket for safe keeping and at the end of the day took it to be identified by an expert in the fossil museum who told me it was an Ichthyosaur vertebrae and that my 'something' was at least ninety million years old!

INSECT (N.)

An invertebrate animal with a well-defined head, thorax and abdomen, three pairs of legs, and typically one or more pairs of wings

J
IS FOR
JOSEPH.
MY FIRST BORN.
SUCH A JOY.

KINSFOLK

(n.) people kindred or related to one another

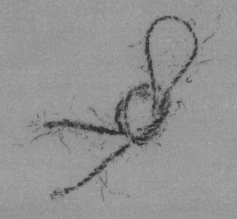

KINSFOLK

(n.) people kindred or related to one another

14.2.87

My husband and I met (on a blind date) at The Captain Digby pub, Kingsgate, Kent. The pub sits right on the edge of the cliff and has done since 1763. The pub's still there, but so far we've never been back.

Kingsgate

knit one, purl one

Kindred Spirits

During a visit to Longleat a male lion
brushed right against our parked car leaving
a muddy smudge. The boys were thrilled!
The car went un-washed for a long time so everyone could admire the evidence of our lucky escape from being a lion's dinner.

legend

lavender today and the scent is divine

dip pen
in lavender
paint — like
the texture

do I like this
purple ink
or not?

MEMORY

(n.) a store of things remembered

I read somewhere that life is a quilt, with each individual day being a seam in a large, pieced cloth. Some seams are awful, some are nice, a few are close to perfect but if you chose to worry over each tiny detail you will miss how colourful, interesting and just plain marvellous the whole blooming thing is.

If any of my quilts are worthy of becoming heirlooms then this is surely the one. So many of our family stories and treasured memories are carefully and thoughtfully stitched into this cloth. I truly loved making my memory quilt but I know the conversations I'll have whilst sitting comfortably under it will be even lovelier.

We are aspiring astronomers and have
spent many a winter's night gazing heavenwards
trying to glimpse distant planets and stars...

MARMALADE TARTLETS

Short crust pastry (made with 6 oz flour, 3 oz fat, etc.)
2 oz each caster sugar and margarine . 1 egg
1 tablespoon fine cake or breadcrumbs
3 tablespoons orange marmalade

Roll out pastry thinly and line a dozen or more patty tins with it. Cut scraps of pastry to make thin strips on top. Put sugar and margarine in a saucepan and melt over a low heat. Remove from heat, add beaten egg, crumbs and marmalade. Mix well, cool, then half-fill prepared tins with the filling. Put strips of pastry crosswise on top and bake for 15 to 20 minutes in a moderately hot oven. *Oven heat 5 or E or 400°F.*

MARSHMALLOW FLAN

28 g

1 sweet flan pastry case baked " blind " (see pastry making) *Shop bought*
42g / 1½ oz butter . 1 oz sugar . 1 tablespoon golden syrup
1 dessertspoon cocoa . 1 teaspoon coffee essence *↓espresso !*
a fairy cake ← 3 good tablespoons cake crumbs
1 tablespoon chopped walnuts . 6 marshmallows *(more)*

Have the pastry cooked and keep it warm. Melt the butter, sugar, syrup, cocoa and coffee essence together in a pan, stir till well-mixed, but do not boil. Remove from heat, add cake crumbs and chopped nuts. Cool slightly, then pour into the pastry case. Place the marshmallows on top, let them melt under a slow grill until they spread, then decorate, if liked, with some halved walnuts.

boys loved this r it was really really easy

MERINGUE FRUIT TART

Short crust pastry (made with 8 oz flour, 4 oz fat, etc.)
1 lb stewed gooseberries . 1 teaspoon cornflour
1 oz plain flour . 5 oz sugar . ½ pint milk . 2 eggs
almond essence . blanched almonds

Line a deep pie-plate with the pastry and bake it " blind " for about 20 minutes. Cook berries with as little water as possible, till tender, but not broken. Place the flour, 2 oz of sugar and milk in a saucepan, blend well and cook till thickening. Cool slightly, add the yolks of the eggs, beaten

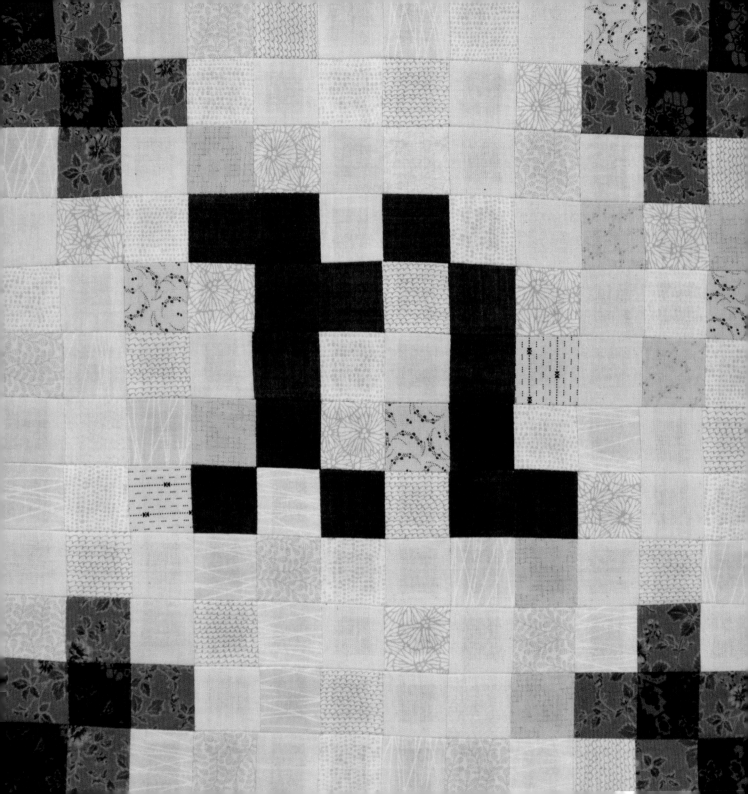

NEW YORK

New York

My birthday is the day before my Mums' and in 2009 we found ourselves about to turn forty and sixty which we both felt were very big numbers to be turning!

We decided to treat ourselves to a little trip to New York and we let my sister come too (even though she didn't have a big birthday to celebrate!) We all shared a room, got very little sleep, ate too much, spent too much and saw all the sights and took in a show on Broadway in a fantastic four day whirlwind trip.

Now fifty and seventy are coming faster than we'd like and we need to start saving and planning for our next big birthday adventure.

Nest

We have two Oak trees in our back garden, which rather conjures up images of rolling lawns and space doesn't it? Sadly, not so!

Our oaks provide a home for bats, squirrels, birds and stag beetles and as Wikipedia has just told me, possibly 284 species of insect too.

We have two Oak trees in our back garden, which rather conjures up images of rolling lawns and space doesn't it? Sadly, not so!

Our oaks provide a home for bats, squirrels, birds and stag beetles and as Wikipedia has just told me, possibly 284 species of insect too.

My Granny kept her face cream in a little
china jar shaped like an owl. You reached
the cream by unscrewing the head and
I remember being pleased with the design
because everyone knows real owls can turn
their heads right round too.

Granny had been gone many years before
I thought of her owl jar again and of course,
no-one had thought to keep it. Thankfully
a quick search of the internet found me one
just like it, and so now I have my own owl
jar sitting on my dressing table.

Mine but sadly never hers.

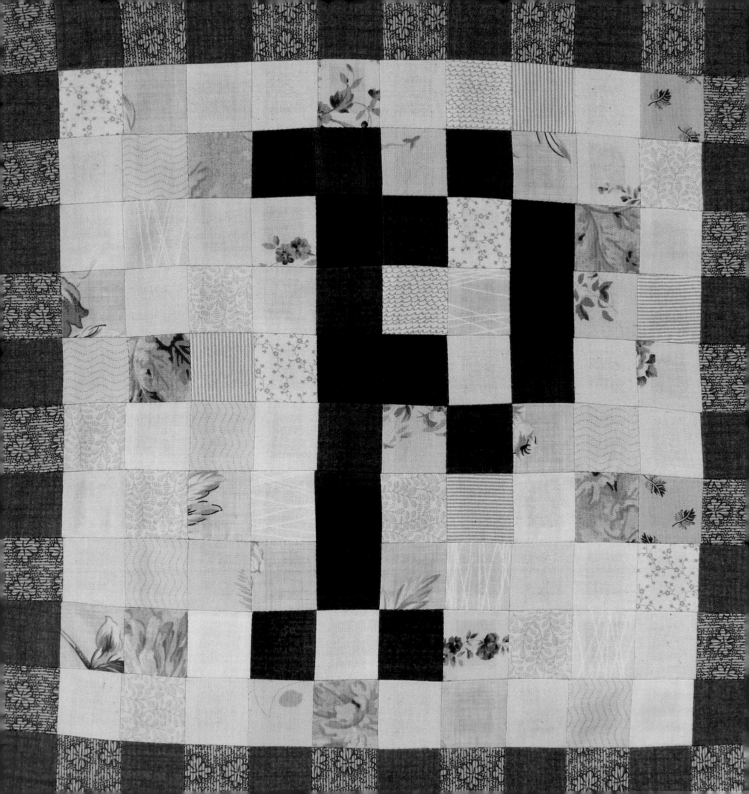

My Uncle Barlow used to race homing pigeons.
I remember waiting with him at the open back door
scanning the skies to see them flying home and how he'd
worry if they were later than expected. He even made his
brother take a pigeon on honeymoon to Scotland with
him so it could have a nice long practice flight home!

plucky

The Poetry Quilt

I'm always jotting down phrases
and sayings I like but rarely
manage to record who actually
said or wrote them, and sadly,
'Warm, sighing quiet settled'
is one such phrase.

So, thank you for the inspiration
dear unknown author: your
charming way with words means
I shall now be sleeping soundly
wrapped in a poem.

To Janet
From Granney

19·78

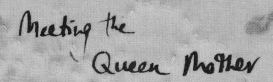

Meeting the Queen Mother

Thirty odd years ago when I was a Girl Guide I was lucky enough to be one of the girls chosen to meet the Queen Mother (now sadly departed) on her visit to Ramsgate, Kent. We were all to stand in line with the other local dignitaries and curtsey to her as she walked from her helicopter along the marina and onto whatever official business had brought her there.

I had the day off school and my parents had me scrubbed, brushed, polished and ironed to within an inch of my life for the occasion. We all stood 'at ease' (but feeling anything but) on the marina waiting and waiting whilst trying to ignore the increasing gale coming off the sea behind us. Long after we all realised the day was not going to plan we were told that the Queen Mum wasn't coming after all because her helicopter couldn't land safely.

We had a hot chocolate in a café on the sea front before heading home feeling pretty fed up. But, I nearly met the Queen Mother and not many people can say that.

run

I used to have a black and white rabbit called
Thruppence (because he cost £3). He never
really warmed to being a pet and was quite
a handful as rabbits go. I loved him though.

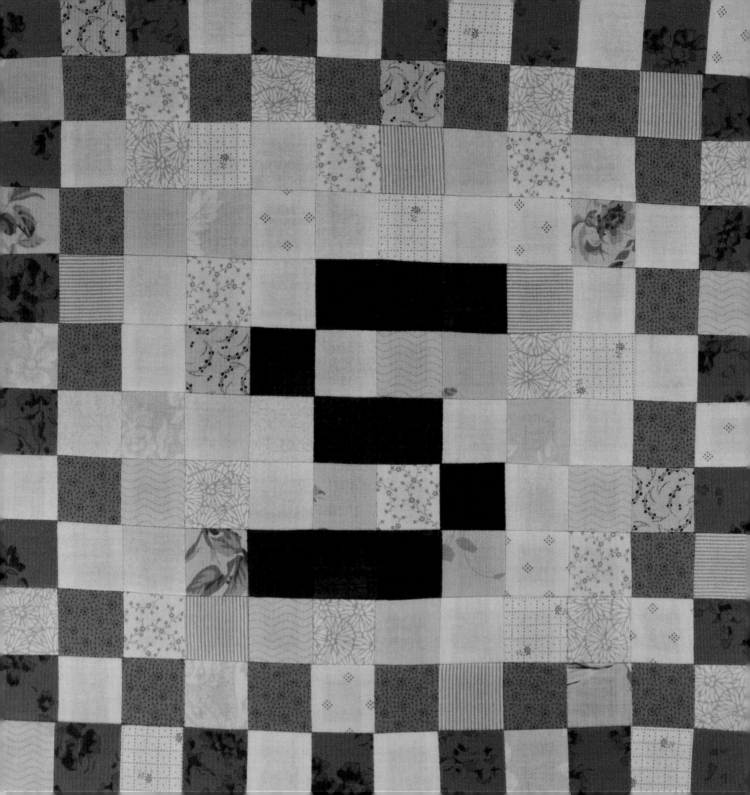

S had to be for Swan because I have two
Swan tales to tell.

1. Our first house was a short walk along the
canal to 'The Swan' pub and we were fairly
frequent visitors there in our pre-children days.

2. Henry has been bitten by a Swan who
mistook his hand for some bread. After the
initial tears Henry was delighted by this turn
of events and has brought it up every time we
have seen a swan since!

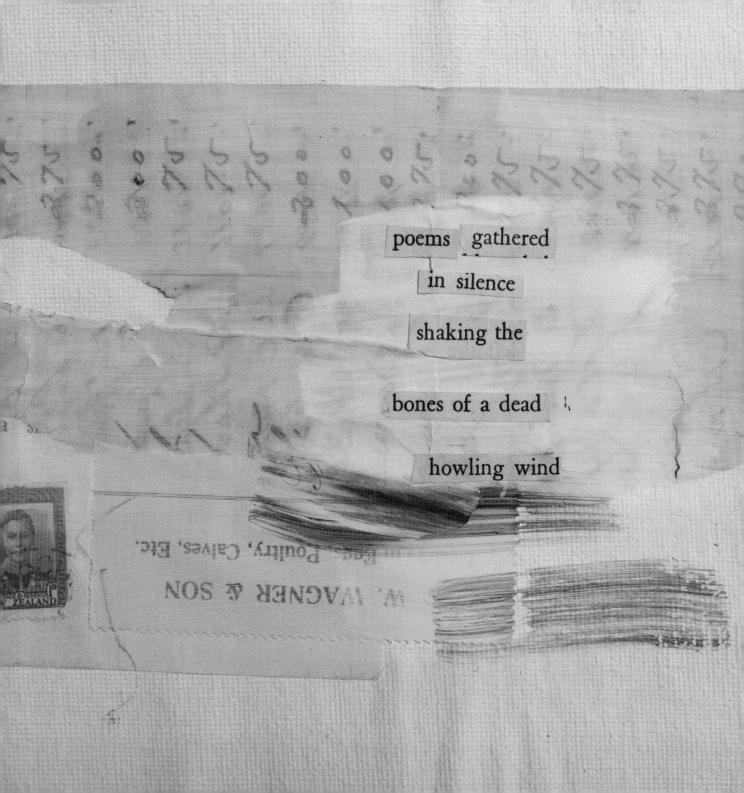

poems gathered

in silence

shaking the

bones of a dead

howling wind

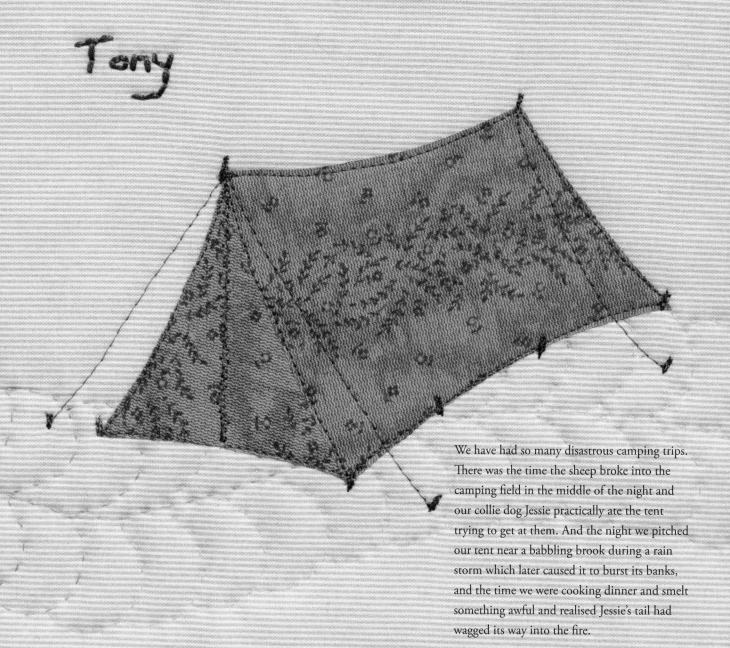

Tony

We have had so many disastrous camping trips. There was the time the sheep broke into the camping field in the middle of the night and our collie dog Jessie practically ate the tent trying to get at them. And the night we pitched our tent near a babbling brook during a rain storm which later caused it to burst its banks, and the time we were cooking dinner and smelt something awful and realised Jessie's tail had wagged its way into the fire.

I won't go on, but I could…

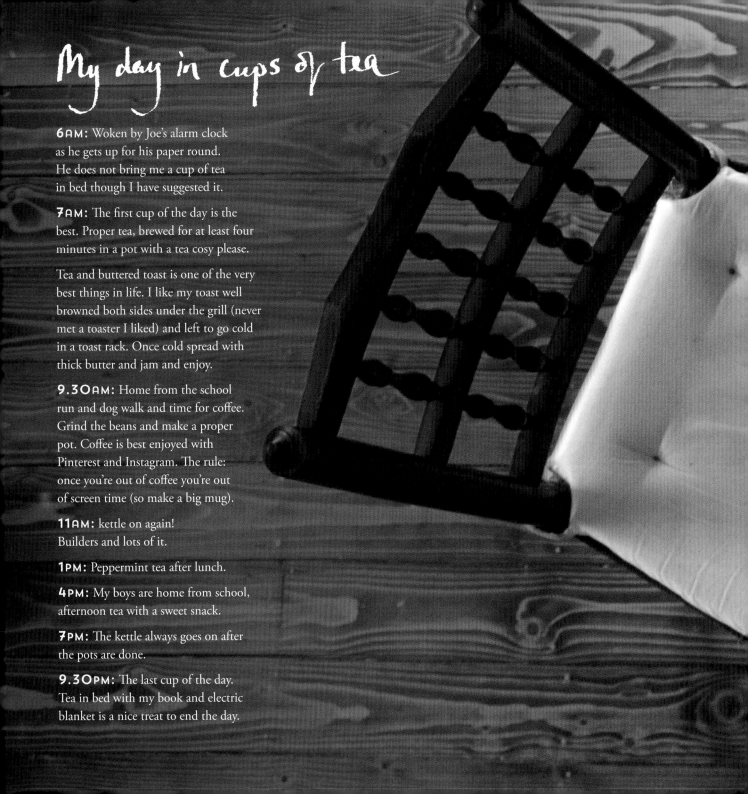

My day in cups of tea

6AM: Woken by Joe's alarm clock as he gets up for his paper round. He does not bring me a cup of tea in bed though I have suggested it.

7AM: The first cup of the day is the best. Proper tea, brewed for at least four minutes in a pot with a tea cosy please.

Tea and buttered toast is one of the very best things in life. I like my toast well browned both sides under the grill (never met a toaster I liked) and left to go cold in a toast rack. Once cold spread with thick butter and jam and enjoy.

9.30AM: Home from the school run and dog walk and time for coffee. Grind the beans and make a proper pot. Coffee is best enjoyed with Pinterest and Instagram. The rule: once you're out of coffee you're out of screen time (so make a big mug).

11AM: kettle on again! Builders and lots of it.

1PM: Peppermint tea after lunch.

4PM: My boys are home from school, afternoon tea with a sweet snack.

7PM: The kettle always goes on after the pots are done.

9.30PM: The last cup of the day. Tea in bed with my book and electric blanket is a nice treat to end the day.

I've worn uniforms to ballet, Guides, school, orchestra and to Saturday jobs.

And perhaps I still do wear one of sorts now; I certainly know what I'm expected to wear at any given event.

These days I'm responsible for my boy's school and Scout uniforms and their team football strips.

You can measure a life by its uniforms.

Valentine

(n.) a person chosen
as a sweetheart

Our Hen is learning the violin and says he loves how it feels under his chin. He sways from side to side when he plays and really enjoys moving his arm gracefully with the bow. Having said that actually getting him to practice in the first place is quite a feat.

Betty the dog always sings along when he's practicing, we're not entirely sure whether it's in pleasure or pain.

My father-in-law was part of a group that tried to rescue a stranded whale once.

The poor thing was found on the Kent coast, miles and miles from where it should have been.

He touched it - and who can say they've done that?

The fabric for this block is very special as it is from my very first collection for 'Moda'

and helped me to achieve a long held ambition.

My father-in-law was part of a group that tried to rescue a stranded whale once.

The poor thing was found on the Kent coast, miles and miles from where it should have been.

He touched it - and who can say they've done that?

The fabric for this block is very special as it is from my very first collection for 'Moda',

and helped me to achieve a long held ambition.

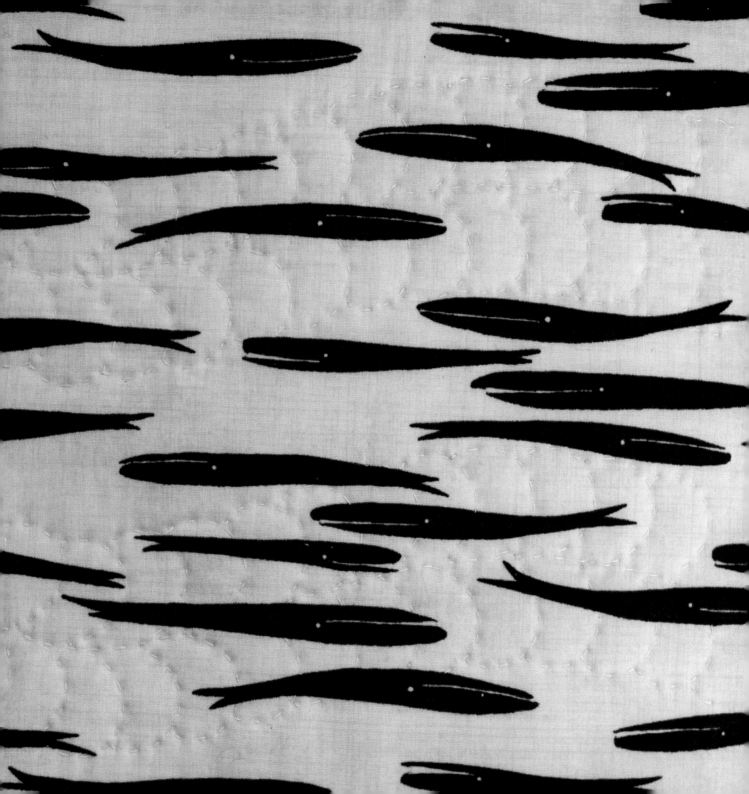

'X' marks the spot.

A written kiss.

What else is there to say
about the letter X?

YEARN

(v.) an intense feeling of longing

YEARN

(v.) an intense feeling of longing

I was lucky enough to visit California as part of a school orchestra exchange.

One of my favourite parts of the trip was the weekend we spent exploring the Yosemite National Park. I've never seen anything like it.

When we were still quite little my sister and I were bridesmaids for our Auntie Liz. I honestly don't remember this at all (and can't believe I'd ever do such a thing) but family legend has it that we sat in the pew behind her entertaining ourselves by trying to un-zip her wedding dress.

Elandslaagte, and relieved Kimberley. On his return he was knighted and was given the command at Aldershot. In 1912 he was made chief of the imperial general staff, and in 1913 a field marshal. In the Great War he commanded the expeditionary forces until Dec., 1915, when he was superseded, a viscounty being conferred upon him in 1916. He took command of the forces in Britain until, in 1918, he was appointed viceroy of Ireland. In 1921 he was made earl of Ypres. He died May 22, 1925.

YSER (Flemish Ijzer). River of France and Belgium. Rising W. of Cassel, dept. of Nord, France, it flows past Dixmude, and enters the North Sea near Nieuport. Its length is 55 m.

The battle of the Yser, fought Oct. 15-31, 1914, was the successful defence against the Germans of the line of the river Yser from Nieuport to Dixmude by the Belgian army with French support.

YTTERBIUM. Rare element. It was discovered in 1878 by Marignac in the mineral gadolinite. In 1907 Urbain announced that he had been able to separate ytterbium by fractional crystallisation into two elements, which he called neoytterbium and lutecium. Its symbol is Yb, atomic weight 173·6, and atomic number 70.

YTTRIUM. One of the metallic elements. Its chemical symbol is Yt, atomic weight 88·9, and atomic number 39. It is a dark grey powder, and is found in gadolinite and other rare earths.

YUCATAN. Peninsula of Central America. It comprises parts of Mexico, British Honduras and Guatemala, and separates the Gulf of Mexico from the Caribbean Sea. It is about 400 m. long and some 200 broad. It contains forests of mahogany, rosewood, and other valuable woods. The peninsula is rich in antiquities.

YUCCA. Genus of plants of the order liliaceae. *See* Adam's Needle.

YUGOSLAVIA. Kingdom of Europe. It comprises the former kingdoms of Serbia and Montenegro with large accessions from Austria and Hungary, among them Bosnia and Herzegovina, and smaller acquisitions from Bulgaria. Its first king was Peter, hitherto king of Serbia, who in 1921 was succeeded by his son Alexander. Belgrade is the capital. It is mainly an agricultural and pastoral country. Minerals include coal, iron, copper and lead. The area is 94,230 sq. m. Pop. (1931) 13,930,918.

On Jan. 6, 1929, King Alexander took the executive power into his own hands. On Feb. 17, 1929, a royal decree brought into being a supreme legislative council of 17 nominated members (11 Serbs, 4 Croats, and 2 Slovenes). In 1931 the constitution was restored and a general election held, but only persons whose names were on a national list could offer themselves for election. The name of the state was changed in 1929 from the kingdom of the Serbs, Croats and Slovenes to the kingdom of Yugoslavia.

YUKON. Territory of Canada. It was made into a separate political unit in 1898, after the discovery of gold on the Klondike. It is bounded by the Arctic Ocean, Alaska, British Columbia, and the North-West Territories. Mt. Logan is 19,540 ft. high; Mt. St. Elias and several other peaks are over 15,000 ft. The chief river is the Yukon, flowing 2,300 m. into the Bering Sea. The area is 207,076 sq. m. Pop. (1931) 4,230.

YURIEV. Russian name of the Estonian town Tartu (q.v.).

Z. Twenty-sixth letter of the English and twenty-fifth of the Latin alphabet. It is a soft sibilant. In the Latin alphabet its use is reserved for Greek words. Its usual English value is that of s in rose.

ZAGREB. Alternative name for the Yugo-Slavian town Agram (q.v.).

ZAMBEZI. River of Africa. It rises in Angola near the headstreams of the Kasai, an affluent of

the Congo, and flows with a great double curve to its mouth in Mozambique. The principal affluent is the Shiré. Its length is some 1,600 m. The Trans-Zambezia rly., 175 m. long, connects Dondo with Murraça. A bridge gives rly. connexion between Nyasaland and Beira.

ZAMORA, NICETO ALCALA. Spanish politician. Born July 6, 1877, he came into prominence as the leader of a party that, in 1930, joined the republicans. He was concerned in the rising of Dec., 1930. When the republic was established in April, 1931, he was head of the provisional government, and in the following December he was elected the first president.

ZANGWILL, ISRAEL British novelist. Born in London, Feb. 14, 1864, of his masterly studies of Jewish life The Children of the Ghetto, 1892, is the best known. His other works include The King of Schnorrers, 1894; The Master, 1895; Dreamers of the Ghetto, 1898; They That Walk in Darkness, 1899; The Mantle of Elijah, 1900. Among his plays are Merely Mary Ann, 1903; The Melting Pot, 1908; Too Much Money 1918. He died Aug. 1, 1926.

ZANTE. One of the Ionian Islands. The chief town is also named Zante. Pop. (1928) 40,492.

ZANZIBAR. British protectorate in E. Africa. It consists of the islands of Zanzibar and Pemba and adjacent small islands. Zanzibar island lies off the N.E. coast of Tanganyika Territory, 25 m. N. of Dar-es-Salaam. The area of Zanzibar island is 640 sq. m. The city has a fine harbour. Pop. (1931) island, 137,741; town, 45,276.

In 1890 the islands became a British protectorate, the coastal strip being divided between Germany, Italy, and Great Britain. The British mainland portion is now the Kenya Protectorate. In 1926 executive and legislative councils were set up, presided over respectively by the sultan and the British resident.

ZARA. Seaport of Italy. It is on the Adriatic Sea, 72 m. N.W. of Spalato (Split), and contains Roman remains and relics of Venetian rule. Before the Great War it was Austrian. Pop. 18,604.

ZARATHUSHTRA. Founder of the religion of ancient Persia and the Parsees, known as Zoroaster (q.v.).

ZEALAND (Danish Sjaelland). Island of Denmark. It lies between the Great Belt and the Sound. To the N. is the Kattegat, and on it is most of Copenhagen. Area 2,680 sq. m.

ZEBRA. Group of animals of the horse family, found only in Africa. They are distinguished by the elaborate black striping on their tawny coats. The common or mountain zebra (Equus zebra) occurs in S. Africa; Grévy's zebra, found in Somaliland and Shoa, is larger than the mountain species. The ground colour of its pelt is almost white, and the stripes are very narrow and numerous. Burchell's zebra (E. burchelli), which is found on the South African plains, resembles the quagga (q.v.).

ZEBRA (Burchell's)

ZEBU (Bos Indicus). Humped race of horned cattle. They are bovine mammals centring in India, but represented by numerous varieties in all tropical countries.

ZEBU

ZECHARIAH. Minor prophet of the Old Testament. He prophesied from the second to the fourth year of Darius Hystaspis. The first six chapters of his book consist of a series of visions dealing with the circumstances of his own time.

ZEDEKIAH. Last king of Judah. The youngest son of Josiah, he was 21 years old when he became king, and his reign lasted for 11 troublous years. His eyes were then put out, and he spent the rest of his life as a prisoner at Babylon.

ZEEBRUGGE. Seaport of Belgium. It lies on the coast, 8 m. by rly. N. of Bruges. A train ferry service with Harwich was opened in 1924. In the Great War the Germans made it a centre of the coastal defences and a submarine base for war on allied shipping.

On the night of April 22-23, 1918, a British naval contingent under vice-admiral Sir R. Keyes dashed into the harbour of Zeebrugge. A landing was effected on the mole to distract attention, while three blockships, filled with cement, were sunk in the canal. The old cruiser, Vindictive, and the ferry boats Iris and Daffodil carried the landing parties, who blew up the viaduct.

ZENANA (Persian, xanana, from zan, woman). Term used for a Hindu harem, i.e. for the apartments in which the women of a family are secluded, and also for the women.

ZENDAVESTA. Name by which the sacred books of the Parsees are known in the West. Correctly, the name should be Avesta and Zend, Law and Commentary. Written originally in Zend, a language allied to Sanskrit, translated into Pahlavi, and later into Parsee, it is attributed to Zoroaster (q.v.).

ZENO (b. 490 B.C.). Greek philosopher. He lived at Elea in Italy, and is remembered as the author of the famous paradoxes of Achilles and the Tortoise and the Arrow.

Another Zeno (c. 340-264 B.C.) was a Greek philosopher, founder of the Stoic school of philosophy, and known as Zeno of Citium.

ZENOBIA. Queen of Palmyra. She was the wife of Odenathus and after his assassination became regent for her son, Vaballath. She occupied Egypt, A.D. 270, and after Aurelian had been defeated by the Goths, she proclaimed her son Augustus. Aurelian, however, defeated her at Emesa. Taken prisoner, she spent her remaining years in retirement at Tibur.

ZEOLITE. In mineralogy, an important group of hydrous silicates of aluminium, sodium, and calcium. The group includes the minerals analcite, laumonite, natrolite, stilbite, and chabazite.

ZEPHANIAH. Minor prophet of the O.T. A son of Cushi, probably of the royal house, his short book deals first with universal judgement for sin, and then briefly with universal salvation.

ZEPPELIN, FERDINAND, COUNT. German airship designer. Born at Constance, July 8, 1838, he joined the army. He retired in 1891, and devoted the remainder of his life to constructing airships of a rigid type. In 1906 he made a successful airship flight of 60 miles in two hours. In 1908 his fourth airship passed the government tests, but was wrecked. A national Zeppelin fund was started, and thereafter numerous airships were built. He died March 8, 1917.

After the Great War a larger ship, the Graf Zeppelin, was built, and in 1932 a still larger one was under construction. *See* Airship.

ZERMATT. Tourist centre of Switzerland. It stands in a valley 22 m. by rly. S. of Visp. Near the base of the Matterhorn and Monte Rosa, it is the starting point of the rly. up the Gornergrat.

ZERO. Mathematical symbol which signifies the absence of quantity or number. It is written 0. In thermometry it is used as one of the fixed points of temperature. Absolute zero (−273° C.) is the temperature at which the molecules of a gas exert no pressure on the sides of a containing

vessel, ...
by 1922 ...
of it by ...

ZETL ...
since 18 ...
baron D ...
this bei ...
3rd earl ...
rence, ...
reputati ...
Ronalds ...
1907-16 ...

ZEUS. ...
identified ...
god of th ...
his chief ...
the oak. ...
Rhea, th ...
Titans a ...

ZIGG ...
diminish ...
The wor ...

ZIMB ...
Bantu na ...
especiall ...
notes th ...
Victoria, ...
1928 an ...
pedition ...
discover ...

ZINC. ...
chemical ...
atomic n ...
crystallin ...
tures, bu ...
which it ...
conducte ...
as spelte ...
sphalerit ...
Red zinc ...

Zinc i ...
the oxid ...
carbon. ...
iron she ...
an alloy ...
silver, ...
employed ...
agent a ...
teries. ...
productio ...
1,280,00 ...
States in ...

ZINNI ...
nual and ...
order co ...
opposite ...
coloured ...

ZION. ...
Jerusalem ...
in a gene ...

ZIONIS ...
Theodor ...
pamphlet ...
Herzl ad ...
mous Jew ...
mandator ...
Organiza ...

ZITHER

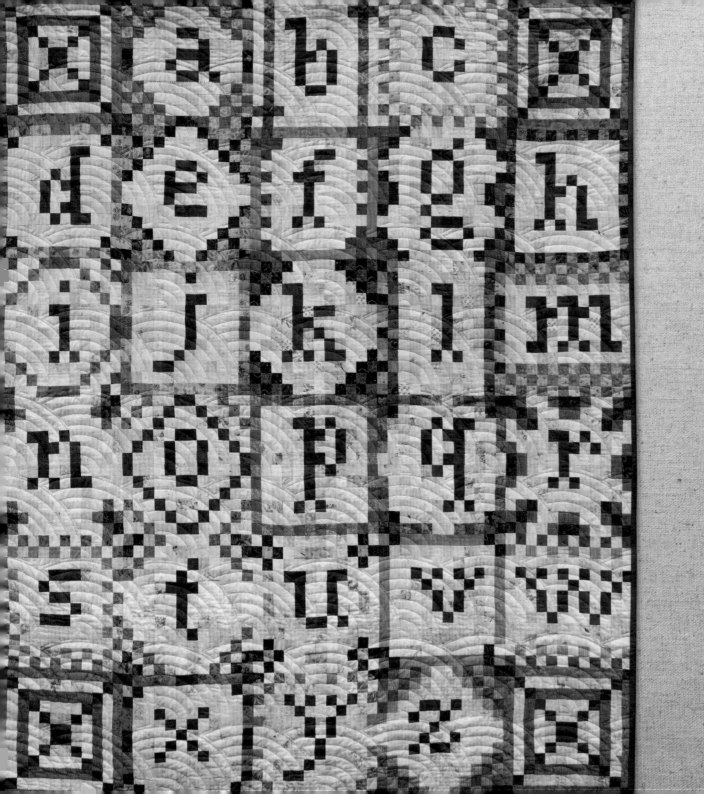

ALPHABET QUILT

FINISHED QUILT MEASURES: 60 x 72 INCHES

There are two types of quilter; those who strive for perfect seams and matching points and can't rest until they get them and those who don't worry about such things and carry on stitching regardless.

By now, you will all realise I am the second kind of quilter and I make no apologies for my mismatched seams because I enjoyed each and every stitch and the finished quilt is stunning (if I do say so myself).

All that is to say, there are 4320 one inch finished squares in this alphabet quilt. So please, please go easy on yourself and just enjoy the stitching!

REQUIREMENTS

Piecing: I used scraps for my 4320 1 ½ inch squares. If you buy fabric for this quilt you will need a total of 6 ½ yards

Letters and corner squares: ¾ yd indigo

Backing: 4 yds

Binding: ¾ yd (cut 3 inches wide)

alphabet quilt

TEMPLATES

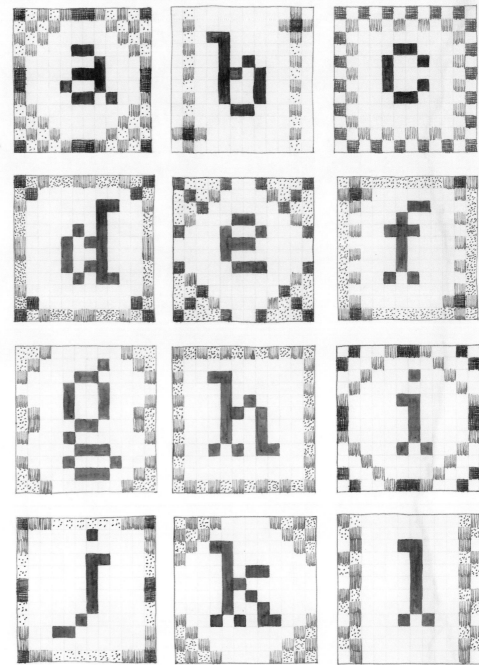

MEMORY QUILT

FINISHED QUILT MEASURES: 40 x 48 INCHES
EACH FINISHED BLOCK MEASURES: 8 x 8 INCHES

These are our stitched family stories and so this memory quilt is unique to us, as yours will be to you. Letters I found tricky may have great significance for you, or you may choose not to use the alphabetical structure at all. Please use what ideas and images you can from my memory quilt but my real hope is that I have inspired and encouraged you to stitch your very own, personal and unique memory quilt.

I chose the 'quilt as you go' method as it enables you to treat each block as a separate entity. This gives you creative freedom and the small scale encourages experimentation. Joining them together at the end is a little fiddly but it's nothing a few evenings sewing, watching films and drinking tea can't sort out!

LITTLE TIPS...

Use a ½ inch seam allowance.

All stitching must be done on the wadding, not in the seam allowances.

When joining the blocks: pin backing fabrics out of the way, align the waddings and stitch fronts with right side together. Stitch the length of the whole seam. The wadding should sit neatly together but not be stitched through. Ensure the front seam allowances inside lie flat over the wadding, trim if needed. Fold one backing fabric seam over the other, turn under the raw edge on the uppermost fabric and slipstitch the seam allowance down. Join the rows of blocks together in the same way.

Before binding: Trim the seams down to the usual ¼ inch or cut your binding wider to accommodate the ½ inch seam allowance. Stitch binding as close to the edge of the wadding as you can.

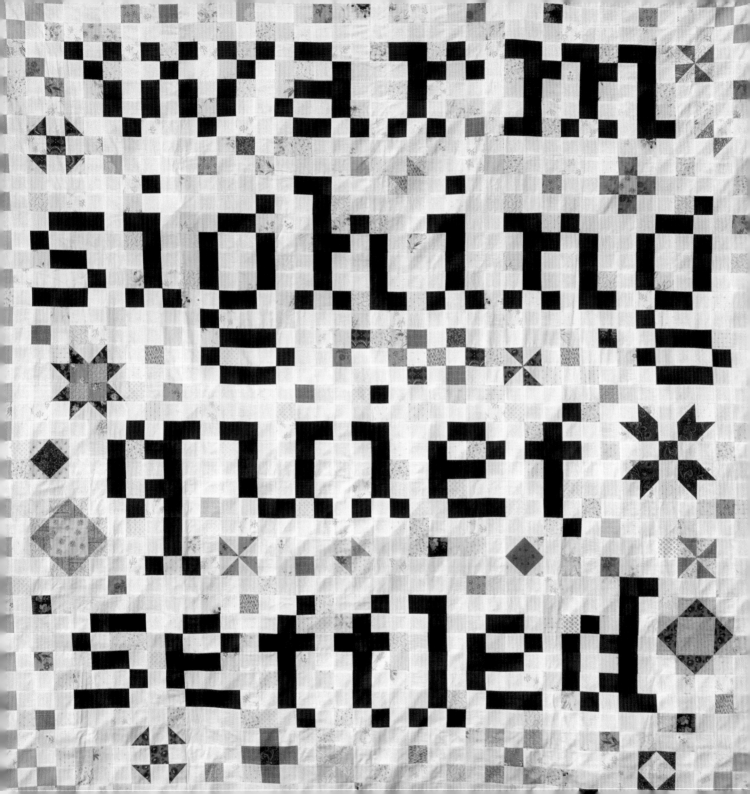

POETRY QUILT

FINISHED QUILT MEASURES: 82 x 90 INCHES

I'd love it if you were inspired to create your own poetry quilt! What's your favourite phrase or saying? If you do choose to design your own poetry quilt you can refer to the individual letter charts for the alphabet quilt. Then take a large sheet of graph paper and carefully add your chosen wording, fill any gaps with traditional pieced blocks and stitch away.

REQUIREMENTS

Piecing: There are a total of 1845 squares (some of which are half square triangle blocks). Cut squares 2 ½ inches. Cut two 2 ⅞ inch squares to make a pair of half square triangles.

Letters: 3 ½ yds (cut 292 indigo 2 ½ inch squares)

Border: 1 ¼ yds (cut 100 grey 2 ½ inch squares)

Backing: 5 yds

Binding: 1 yd (cut 3 inches wide)

INSTRUCTIONS

I found it easier to sew this quilt in blocks of ten squares by ten rows, whether or not these included half of a pieced block or letter.

Please refer to the chart for the layout. Keep your cut squares as neatly organised as you can and chain piece methodically and all will be well.

Janet Clare

OTHER TITLES AVAILABLE...

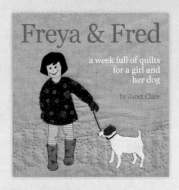

FREYA & FRED
ISBN: 978-0-9569770-0-7

HEARTY GOOD WISHES
ISBN: 978-0-9569770-1-4

A FIELD GUIDE
ISBN: 978-0-9569770-2-1

HAYLEY

Graphic design, layout and
all technical computer bits.
H turns our work into a real book.

JANET

Sewing, drawing,
writing & daydreaming.

SARAH

Stylist, set dressing and
photography. Basically, she
makes my work look good.

THE WORDSMITH TEAM

we're
never far
from a pot
of tea

 **SARAH**

Stylist, set dressing and
photography. Basically, she
makes my work look good.

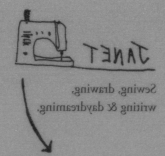 **JANET**

 **HAYLEY**

Graphic design, layout and
all technical computer bits.
H turns our work into a real book.

THE WORDSMITH TEAM

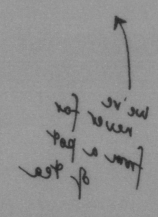

we've
never for
from a pot
of tea

MY THANKS GO TO...

You just can't make a book like this all by yourself and so I am truly grateful for all the hard work and care given to 'The Wordsmith' by these lovely ladies and gentlemen: I couldn't (and wouldn't) want to do it without you x

TONY: my chief of everything.

SARAH: for all your marvellous pictures, child wrangling and all round loveliness.
www.sarahegginton.co.uk

HAYLEY: who takes my words, drawings and ideas and transforms them into a real and beautiful book. Graphic designer extraordinaire!
www.hayleybush.co.uk

RICHARD: just the best and nicest printer.
www.colourstream.com

And lastly, thank you Megan Young for 'Sorrow' the found poem. We have yet to meet but I know we'd get on like a house on fire.
www.thescentofwater.typepad.com

FREE PATTERNS | SEWING TIPS | BLOG | SHOP

www.janetclare.co.uk

any questions? Email me: janet@janetclare.co.uk